Poetry: in the Search of 42

by Fern Renee

ASTERIA
BOOKS

Poetry: in the Search of 42

by Fern Renee

Project Editor: Laurelei Black
Cover Artist by: River Routen

Fern Renee
Poetry: In the Search of 42.
ISBN 978-0-9857734-7-2
EAN-13
Keywords
1. poetry collection 2. personal transformation 3. feminism
Copyright © 2020 by Asteria Books

Table of Contents:

An Open Letter to My Abusers

Fuck you.
From the little girl that was taught by your actions that
love is used to hurt,
that kindness and affection are things not to trust.

Fuck you.
From the teenager who let the boys touch her, because
that was the way
she was trained. be quiet, stay still, say no and you will be
hurt. Take it and
like it 'cause you're just a whore anyway, and worth
nothing more.

Fuck you.
From the young woman moving into motherhood with a
man that says he
loves her, but will still not hear her when she tries to say
no. it's my duty as
wife to please my husband. so she never does, and cries
herself to sleep
more nights than not. who kept telling herself that maybe
if SHE was just
better it would be ok.

Fuck you.
From the woman who finally left and is starting over; all
the way over;
from the beginning over. Because she never found out
who she was because
the moment you touched her and stole her innocence and
ripped off her

crown and fed her the lie of a slave, no worth but what
you gave, no breath
but what you saw fit to give.

Fuck you.
From me.
The woman who is here, streaked with the bloody mess
of my rebirth.
I hold my crown high upon my head.
Self Sovereign.
Queen.
and I say again.
FUCK YOU.

Oracle

If you find it hard to speak,
come whisper in my ear,
spill tears on my shoulder
and seethe into the dark.
If your voice has been
silenced, and the words
will not come, I will share your
quiet and drink in your strength.
and I will Rage at the world
in your stead.
I will scream to the heavens
that you and I demand to be
heard, that the crimes
against our very souls
be Witnessed.
If you can not speak
I will scream,
If you can not whisper
I will rage,
If you can not stand
I will carry you
We will be heard
and we will be healed.

Rise

We have been made
to forget the value
of our worth.
that is its tied up in
how much skin is shared
how much is shown.
it has been swept under
the carpets of covering
everyone's scars with love
and leaving their own
to heal in jagged ruin.
It is time to wake up,
it is time to pull out of
the mire of the lost ages
to become that which we
were always meant to be,
Goddess all.

Beautiful Destruction

Apocalypse seems eventual
the ever-flowing stream
of the woes of the world
the woes of ourselves
the pain and chaos
of our world gone mad,
but not the whole big world
with all of its woes,
the one of our own making
the one that is there that we
make every day, with every breath,
every thought and choice.
When that slips into chaos
and we learn the hard truths
that shatter the illusion
and we rage and scream
and bleed tears at the loss of
the beauty that we held so dear,
and when the tears slow and the
light starts to come back through
and we can see the reflection of
what was underneath and in
its beauty left speechless.

Listen

Can you hear me?
Does my voice make it through
the haze of worthlessness that
you descend into when the darkness comes?
Can you make out the whispers
that I am here with you and even
in this darkness, I stay?
Will you understand the sounds
that fall from my lips
as I scream to you
that I love you?
Can you hear me
when I tell you
you are not alone?

Tick Tock

It is time.
Time to stop.
Stop hiding and
Shine Brightly
to bring forth
the flame that
illuminates the
shadows so
they may be seen
and learned.

It is time.
Time to face it,
Face our own
darkness, embrace
and dance with it
pull it out of the shadows
and show it the beauty of
the light that creates it.

Trailing Off

Do you seek
    oblivion in
        my eyes, or
    a reflection
of what
    might be?
      Temptation, speaks
as soft as a feather
      falling. Is it your
          redemption or
            just the path
               to perdition?

Whispered Teachings

My muse is dancing
again, skillfully moving
twisting and swaying
lips to ears, spilling
things to send shivers,
to make me want,
to make me feel.
Touch -- she says, --
taste, and drink in
the scent of you.

I wonder at its
flavor and my thoughts
drift into places
they haven't been
in so long.

And I want,
to feel again,
to be felt again,
whispered to and
left to sigh in
trembled anticipation.

Lamp Light

Where is the lantern,
left out for me, to find my
way back inside to my
hearth, my soul, me?
Sometimes it feels like
the snuffer has been set,
capped on the wick, the shutters
closed, where the key to unlock
the glass, to tear the walls
from the flame, to
see it and feel it,
to dance and smile
the spin of the heat
to waken my being
to maybe warm your
arms, for a while to
pass the shaking of
sorrows extinguishing tears.

In a Lifetime Past

I
was nothing
but
a novelty,
something to try
something to be
nothing I have is what you want
nothing I can give is what you need
memories build up over and over
laughter, and joyfulness
but that was before,
and
I was new,
and
now I'm old.
My light has faded from your eyes,
and
I am
left once again in
your blindness,
grasping and reaching
and just getting pushed back.
I can't win against this
you don't want me to.
So I go back
to what I once was --
nothing
and nothing
I will be
but a novelty.

Truth Within

So many of the things
that fall from fingers
to drift into the pages
of unforgotten words
have often been said
before, by hearts broken
the same, lovers embraced
of the same arms.
By the politics of madmen,
and the truth of liars.
But somehow, somewhere
along the way, the tenor
changed and they
became my own, and
they became yours
and then, sweet bliss
they became real.
Again, they became truth,
again. But this time
it was me and it was you
that spoke them,
and it was you and I
that listened.

Mother

Memory lost, like tears
in the rain. So many frail
things kept safe, except
from the hands that you
never restrained.

The innocence lost, stolen,
and broken by the
name of God on
the lips of children,
left me wanting
a new deity, a new
place to seek haven.

And so without tears
of parted sorrow, I said
never again. The space you
held left vacant, I boarded up
the doorway, your image
lost and forgotten.

I am my own Goddess
now, and no longer need
your words, I am no longer
the sacrificial lamb left
to the altars of your
broken soul.

Dark Waters

Like little claws
they whisper in
my mind, so I
fill my ears with
music, my thoughts
with liquid nothing
sound from others'
fingers, others' muses
speak to me, to
pull me from this
place of shadowed
thoughts, and unwanted
atrocities, faith and trust
love and so much more
fragile things to be
batted about in
my often too turbulent
sea of mixed things
the tears of salted
memories.
When all I call for
is the harpoon, the knife
the bullet to the head.
Drown it all away,
who needs the things I
have when the doubts
of an unsure heart
will twist it, like a
maelstrom in the sea?

Lily White

The *flowers* you gave me
had *razor* blade cuts
on the stems, as if
they didn't want to
let go of the life they had.
I wanted to put *stitches*
over them to bring them
back to life, but the *throats*
of those beauties kept
spilling milk, over my hands
and I couldn't keep them alive
long enough to love them.

Lullaby

Shhhhh

The wind whispered
cool against my neck,
eyes closed and thoughts
bared to the air,
a sigh, lost from
lips, as she
pleaded..
don't go.

While slumber beckons
with smooth arms, and
truly entrancing lips,
darkness slips from skin
to cover my eyes
and for a time,
I find a dream close
enough to touch, and only
barely whisper it
to the wind, for
fear it will
flee from lasting
scars.

Autumnal Kisses

It's there in the wind
the touch that chills
and sends me to that
place of expectant expectations,
the twist in the sky that
speaks of the days
to come, when fabric
alone cannot warm
the soul, that fingertip
smiles and reaching
arms must fill the
space that the leaves
once lived, as they turn
in the dance that She
moves to as the Wheel
turns another notch.
Another tick in the time
of falling, falling, like
the tears in Her eyes.
Golden rust that fills
the air, speaking in
hushed tones, the
silence of the
death of season.

Prayer

Oh Mother Sun
how I have missed
your touch, fire
upon flesh, searing
the blue tinges
from my lips
and flushing skin
too white,
consume this
husk, Mother
please, let me
go, set me
free.

Withered in the Sun

She gasps for water,
for air that doesn't burn,
the need to keep going
there are parts of her
that have to go on, places for
her feet to see, though
rooted to the ground
she is, and it is like bones
in the sun, desiccating her arms
and withering her face as she
holds it up to the sun,
praying for just a drop of
water, a cloud to pass over her
sky and rain the tears that dried
up on her face so long ago.

Premonition

Tangled between the
ever present now
and the maybe
that haunts my
dreams, I am no
longer able to look
the future in the
eyes for fear it
won't ever let me in.

You

Would it matter
if the words I write
are just for you,
would the difference be
that not everyone feels
this way, that it's
special because I wrote
them, or would you
think that the things
I say, and feel are just
thoughts and not meant
to be kept by anyone
but me. It's my ink
that stains these papers,
my thirst that needs to
be quenched.

But it's you,
that make it so.

About Fern Renee
A Glimpse at the Poet

Fern Renee has been
writing poetry, prose,
and short stories since
her teen years. She is
the mother of three
humans and two
canines, currently
living in the woods of
rural Indiana.

www.neverthegreyer.tumblr.com

www.facebook.com/greymusings

www.greyhaime.wordpress.com

www.ingramcontent.com/pod-product-compliance
Lightning Source LLC
Chambersburg PA
CBHW020448030426
42337CB00014B/1462